D1214705

FIRST STEPS IN BALLET

FIRST STEPS IN **ballet**

BASIC BARRE EXERCISES FOR HOME PRACTICE

BY **Thalia Mara**

WITH LEE WYNDHAM

ILLUSTRATED BY GEORGE BOBRIZKY

DOUBLEDAY & COMPANY, INC., GARDEN CITY, NEW YORK

ISBN: 0-385-02432-0

Library of Congress Catalog Card Number 55-6550

15   14   13   12

FOREWORD: TO PARENTS

This little book, while explicit in details and analysis of basic ballet barre exercises, is not intended as a guide to self-instruction. It has been written as an aid to intelligent practice at home for the ballet student. As such I believe that it meets a genuine need and demand.

Many parents are distressed at what they feel is a lack on the part of their children in not wanting to practice at home the things they have been learning in ballet class. However, most conscientious teachers do not like to have beginners practice at home because they feel that the beginning student can do himself more harm than good by repeating incorrectly the exercises he does not yet understand.

The study of ballet should be undertaken only under the expert guidance of a really competent teacher. Even if these exercises seem very clear to you or your child I strongly urge against self-instruction. The bones of a young child are soft and malleable. The tendons and muscles of the feet and legs interlace with those of the back and it is the correct use of these tendons and muscles pulling against each other which build the strength and shapeliness of the ballet dancer. A good teacher knows all of these things and how to balance the exercises to develop the results of grace, beauty, and poise.

Incorrect repetition of the details of these same exercises can have a disastrous effect on the feet, back, and muscular development of the legs.

For these same reasons I urgently advise you to be certain that your child is studying under a bona fide teacher of ballet—one who understands the principles of body placement, who knows the correct balance of the basic exercises of ballet and carefully supervises their correct execution by the individual student in the class.

If you are in doubt as to how to choose a teacher of the proper qualifications, be guided by the answers to these questions:

1. What is the teacher's background? It should include at least four or five years of intensive and concentrated study under a recognized ballet master. Professional experience does not always mean that the teacher is an expert on ballet. There are many kinds of dancing in the professional theater. If your teacher's background includes performing in a ballet troupe, you are very fortunate, as this experience will aid in developing artistry in your child. However, a teacher with a good solid background of earnest study under recognized ballet masters is preferable to one who may have had years of theatrical experience but little training in the fundamentals of ballet

technique. While there are many good ballet teachers who belong to organizations of dancing teachers membership in such an organization does not necessarily mean that the teacher is qualified to teach ballet.

2. What does the teacher claim to teach? Today "ballet" is a magic word—one that spells glamour and beauty to hundreds of thousands of little girls and their parents. Many people profess to teach ballet who really do not have the proper background of training for the job. If your child is studying ballet because you wish her to have the advantages of increased grace, poise, beauty of posture, and sound symmetrical muscular development, then what you want her to have is *academic classical ballet technique*.

3. Does the teacher accept children of any age for ballet training? Ballet experts everywhere in the world agree that children under eight years of age should not begin technical training in ballet. The reasons for this are both physical and psychological. Of course there have been a few notable exceptions to this rule—very gifted ballerinas who began at a younger age. But such exceptions are very rare and in any case there is nothing to be gained by starting the child too soon and much may be lost.

Physically the technical exercises of ballet, if performed correctly, are too severe for the very soft bones of children under eight years of age. There is too much strain on the knees and the back. Mentally the child is incapable of the concentration required to understand the details of correct execution. If the exercises are performed incorrectly permanent damage may be done to the feet and muscular structure of the legs.

There is also the danger that real talent may be destroyed by forcing the immature little mind into something for which it is not ready. Ballet is a very disciplined art. While it provides an interesting and even fascinating challenge to the child old enough to appreciate and grasp its principles, such discipline is too exacting for the very young child who needs more freedom of thought and expression.

Children from four to eight years may very profitably study dancing, but it should be a form of dance based on rhythmic exercises, movements for co-ordination and grace, and little dances based on nursery rhymes and fairy tales. Such preballet training is excellent to prepare them for the study of actual ballet technique. Under no circumstances should they be permitted to dance "on toe."

4. Does the teacher use a graded system? A really good teacher uses a graded system in teaching, beginning with the most basic fundamentals and advancing by stages to more difficult and complicated exercises, steps, and combinations of steps. This system may be the teacher's own if he or she has had sufficient background and ex-

perience to evolve such a system, or it may be the system of some famous teacher or master.

There are three distinct schools of technique in ballet: the Russian, the Italian (also called Cecchetti), and the French. The teacher may base his system entirely on the theories of one school or on a combination of the theories of Russian-Italian, or Russian-French, etc. My own preference, based on my professional experiences both as a dancer and as a teacher, is for a combination of the Russian-Italian theories. The Italian to give strength, balance, and perfect co-ordination of the legs, arms, torso, and head, and the Russian to give grace and a larger sense of freedom in movement.

5. What is the teacher's viewpoint on "toe dancing"? Beware of the teacher to whom "ballet" means only "toe dancing." Dancing on the tips of the toes is the very ultimate in ballet technique for the ballerina. It's study should not be begun until after at least two or three years of consistent study and practice in the basic exercises of ballet. When sufficient strength has been built in the feet, legs, and back of the child, so that she can stand on the *demi-pointes* perfectly "placed," with her knees tightly pulled up and the weight lifted up from her feet, so that her toes do not bear the dead weight of her body, then she is ready to begin dancing *sur les pointes*, or on her toes.

6. Does the teacher treat ballet as a separate subject? A great many teachers, particularly those in the smaller towns throughout the country, must include in the curriculum of their schools a variety of dancing such as ballet, tap, acrobatic, ballroom, etc. There is no reason why they should not. However, tap and other types of dance must be taught in classes separate from ballet. No real teacher who knows and understands ballet will teach it in combination with other subjects—such as twenty minutes of ballet, twenty minutes of tap, and twenty minutes of acrobatic. Nothing constructive can be gained or accomplished in this manner.

A ballet class should consist entirely of ballet technique and should be one hour in length. Later, as the student advances and becomes stronger, classes may be lengthened to one and one half hours, but for children one hour is sufficient. Each class should be partitioned into barre work, port de bras, center barre, adagio, and allegro. A beginner should spend thirty or forty minutes of the hour at the barre in order to acquire the "placement," strength, and balance necessary to execute the center work correctly.

Don't be misled by phrases such as "modern methods" or "old-fashioned methods." This is usually a cover-up for ignorance of true methods.

Having placed your child in the school of your choice, do all you can to encourage her by taking an active interest in her work. Be sure to attend visitors' days at the school, so that she can look forward to your approval of her progress. However, do observe the good-conduct rules for parents by doing nothing to distract the child's attention from her teacher, even if she is not doing as well as you think she should. Show your respect for the teacher by allowing her (or him) to do the teaching and do not try to impose your ideas on how the class should be conducted.

Help your little would-be ballerina at home by checking her in her practice sessions for correct posture, placement, etc. Above all—be patient! It takes many years of effort and persistence to make a dancer or acquire the grace and poise you long to see your child display.

One final word—although the illustrations of this book are feminine and addressed mainly to girls, I would like to point out that ballet is not just a feminine art. Actually it began as a masculine art and it is still a manly and fine art for boys in spite of the popular misconception that it is "sissy." As anyone who has seen a ballet performance knows, there is nothing more thrilling than the performance of a fine male dancer.

Ballet requires the strength of an athlete, but is twice as difficult as athletics because the strength must be concealed by ease of movement. It is no more "sissy" than any type of athletics. In fact many coaches are sending their basketball and football team members to ballet classes to learn co-ordination. Famous boxing stars have studied ballet to improve their footwork. It's time American boys and their parents overcame this silly attitude. Studying the arts will not make a "sissy" out of any boy who is not already one. If you would like your son to develop a strong, healthy body, good physical and mental co-ordination, an appreciation of music, painting, literature, and drama—send him to ballet class!

Thalia Mara

SCHOOL OF BALLET REPERTORY, NEW YORK

NOTE TO STUDENTS

If you love the art of ballet and really want to make progress in learning its technique, you must be very faithful about attending your lessons and keeping your practice schedule.

Do not miss classes for any reason except illness and do not allow anything to interfere with your practice schedule. Set aside certain hours of certain days as practice hours. Practice slowly and carefully. Each time pick out one or two exercises you feel need particular attention and work to improve them.

Remember that even famous dancers who have been dancing since *they* were children still repeat these same barre exercises daily. If you think of all the details you are trying to get right, and of how each time you practice correctly you gain a little strength and a little ease, so that you can soon go on to more difficult and interesting steps, you will never be bored by repeating the same exercises.

If possible try to have one place in which to practice. If you are lucky enough to have a playroom or a large enough bedroom, perhaps you can persuade your dad to put up a little practice barre—the wooden rail should be about 2 inches in diameter and may be secured to the wall (about 2½ or 3 feet above the floor) with brackets and screws. The height of the barre depends upon your height and may be judged according to the position of your hand on the barre as in Illustration Number 64. If you cannot have a special barre the footboard of your bed or the back of a chair or a stair railing will do nicely. The floor should be bare and unwaxed.

Practice for about twenty or thirty minutes each time. It is better to practice seriously for a shorter period of time than to fool around for an hour. Of course the more often you practice the more you will improve, but you will have to work this out according to your own schedule of school, homework, playtime, dancing lessons, piano lessons.

It is very helpful to have music to practice to and this is important to develop your sense of rhythm and timing. If you have a phonograph you may obtain special records for the barre-work practice I have outlined in this book from the Selva-Ringle Record Company, 1607 Broadway, New York City. They may be ordered directly by mail or obtained through your teacher. Ask for the Red Label Ballet Series records Numbers 101, 102, and 103.

It should inspire you to remember that every great ballerina and every great *premier danseur* in every country in the world has studied and practiced these very same exercises just as you are doing now. If you are as faithful to your work as they were, perhaps you too may reach the stars!

CONTENTS

POSTURE AND PLACEMENT

The very first thing a would-be ballet dancer must learn is how to stand properly. When we hold our bodies correctly all the steps and exercises are easier to do and they look better. In ballet we call this "correct body placement."

Remember that in practicing the exercises and steps of ballet the important thing is to practice slowly and to try to improve details. It is better to practice one thing correctly with proper attention to the details of correct placement than just to go through the motions of half a dozen exercises halfheartedly or incorrectly.

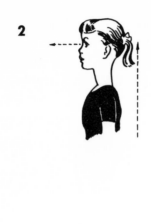

POSTURE—STAND LIKE THIS!

1. Pull your seat under and the stomach up so your back is flat and straight. Lift up your ribs so your chest feels high.

2. Keep your chin up and your head straight. Open your eyes and look straight out.

3. Press the shoulder blades down so your neck looks long and graceful. Allow the shoulders to remain in their natural position; don't force them back.

4. Stand with your weight forward over the balls of your feet so that your heels feel free although they remain on the floor. Try not to feel stiff. Even though you feel very lifted up, breathe deeply and easily and try to feel easy.

5. 6. 7. Don't stand like this!

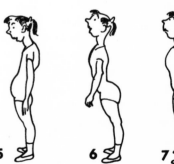

CORRECT BODY PLACEMENT

Correct posture is an important part of body placement. Here are other things to remember if you want to be properly "placed."

8. Lifting: Lift yourself up out of your hips so your body feels as long as possible. Pull up your thigh muscles so your knees are very straight. This keeps you from being dead weight on your feet.

9. Centering: Now imagine that there is a line that starts at the crown of your head and goes straight down your middle, ending between your feet. This is your "axis."

Imagine another line that goes straight across your hips. Both hips must always remain even and straight.

In everything that you do, no matter how you move, don't get "off center." That is, do not allow your body to lean out of line on its axis. When you point your foot out or raise it up, be sure your hips stay in the straight line; don't let one hip get higher than the other.

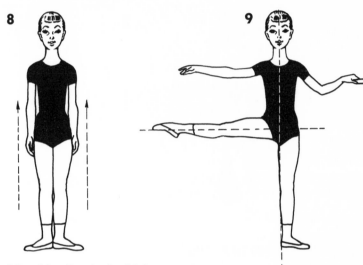

8 9

10. 11. Don't do this!

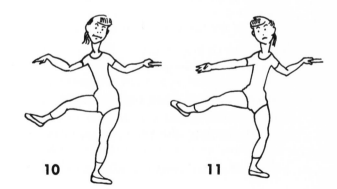

10   11

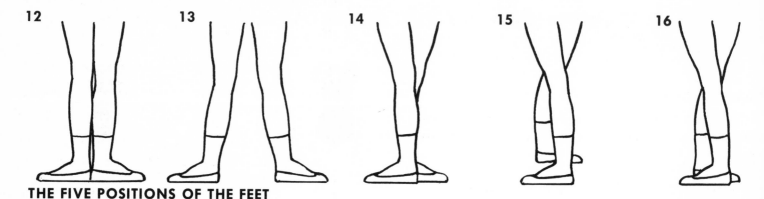

THE FIVE POSITIONS OF THE FEET

Here are the correct positions of the feet with the full 180° turn-out:

12. First Position. Heels touching. Legs opened outward at the hip so that the feet are turned out and make a straight line from the toes of the right foot to the toes of the left foot. Both knees straight.

13. Second Position. Feet are about a foot apart, weight even over both feet. Legs and feet turned outward as in First Position. Both knees straight.

14. Third Position. Both legs are opened outward from the hips, and the heel of the right foot is placed in front of the arch of the left foot. The feet touch. The weight is distributed evenly over both feet. Both knee straight.

15. Fourth Position. Both legs are opened outward from the hips. The feet are about one foot apart with the right foot opposite the left foot and directly in front o it (heel of the right foot in front of the toes of the lef foot). Both knees straight, the weight evenly distrib uted over both feet.

16. Fifth Position. Both legs opened outward from the hips. The heel of the right foot is in front of the joint of the big toe of the left foot. The feet touch at al points and the knees are straight. The weight is evenly distributed over both feet.

This full turn-out of the feet cannot be achieved immediately and if you try to force your feet to turn out fully you will injure them. Your turn-out must come at the hip joint—the entire leg must be opened outward from the hip.

17. 18. 19. 20. 21. Here are the five positions again with the right degree of turn-out for a beginner. Open your legs as far outward as your hips will allow and do not force your feet to turn out further. Turning out more than you are able from your hips is a great strain on your knees and feet. If you practice your barre exercises correctly and conscientiously, the ligaments at your hips will stretch and become limber and your turn-out will improve until you can turn your legs easily and without any strain.

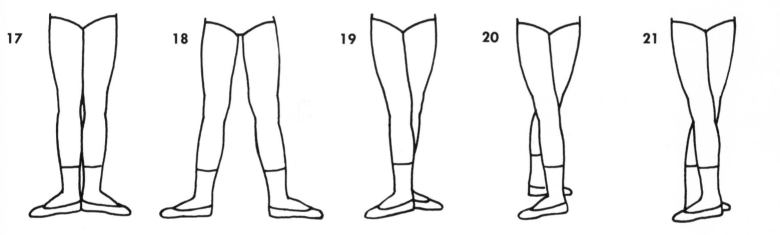

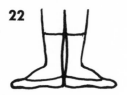

22. Be sure that your foot is always straight and that all the toes are on the floor at all times. If you force your feet to turn out more than you are able to turn from the hip it will cause the feet to roll inward on the arches and can result in much damage to your feet. Be sure that as you stand, whether you are on two feet or one foot, you hold the floor firmly with the little toe and the big toe. The heel should be aligned (in line) with the toes. Grip the floor lightly with all the toes so that the instep or arch is lifted up.

23. Don't do this. The little toe has been allowed to leave the floor and the foot is rolled inward.

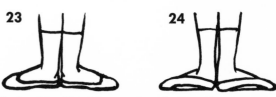

24. Don't do this. The big toe has been allowed to leave the floor and the foot is rolling outward.

THE DEMI-PLIÉ   (deh'-mee plee-ay')

Your very first exercise at the barre is the *demi-plié*. It is most important for you to master this and later the *grand plié*, because the *plié* is the basis of everything you do in ballet. Practically all of the steps of ballet use the *plié* in some degree. In jumping steps it is the good *demi-plié* that gives the effect of lightness to your jumping. That is what is called *ballon*—a bouncy, light quality in all the leaping and bounding steps.

Although the *plié* may be done facing at right angle to the barre and holding it with one hand, it is a good idea to face the barre, when you practice, and hold it with both hands. This will help you to hold your back straight and to keep your shoulders straight front. Stand about six inches away from the barre, or at a comfortable distance so that you do not have to reach out; don't be too close, because that will make your shoulders hunch and spoil your position.

Under each set of illustrations of the *demi-plié*, in the different positions, I have given you some things to remember to do and some to remember not to do. These instructions are not just for the *demi-plié* in that particular position, but are meant for all the positions.

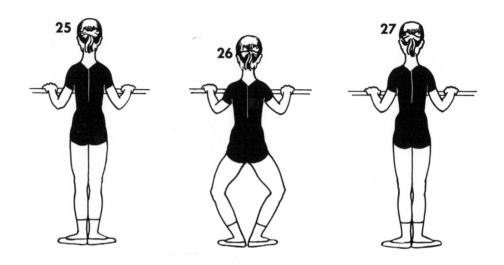

DEMI-PLIÉ IN FIRST POSITION

25. Ready. Bend the knees to the count: 26. "And one, and two . . ." 27. Straighten the knees to the count: "And three, and four."

The timing of the *plié* is very important. Do not bend the knees quickly and do not straighten them quickly. Take two slow counts to bend them, and then two slow counts to straighten them.

Keep the heels firmly on the floor. The *demi-plié* i especially useful to stretch the tendons at the back o the heels, so you must remember not to allow th heels to leave the floor no matter in which positio you do the *demi-plié*. Keep the spine very straight the shoulders low. Be very, very careful not to si into your hips. Lift up out of them.

DEMI-PLIÉ IN SECOND POSITION

28. Ready.   29. "And one, and two."   30. "And three, and four."

Remember to turn out your whole leg from the hip in all these positions. Do not force your feet to turn out further than the entire leg can turn. Keep ALL of the toes on the floor, do not roll forward on your instep so that the little toe leaves the floor, and do not roll out so that the big toe leaves the floor. Hold the floor firmly with the toes so that you can feel the arches lift. Press the knees outward over the toes, do not allow them to fall forward in front of the arches.

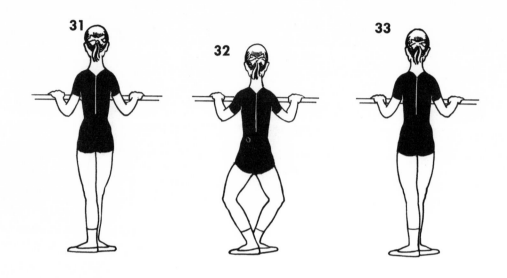

DEMI-PLIÉ IN THIRD POSITION

31. Ready. 32. "And one, and two." 33. "And three, and four."

The Third Position is not often used in ballet now-adays. However, if your legs are naturally rather turned in and you find the turn-out in Fifth Position impossible to achieve without strain and rolling in on the insteps, then practice Third Position rather than Fifth for this exercise. Proceed exactly as for Fifth Position in bending and straightening the knees.

DEMI-PLIÉ IN FOURTH POSITION

34. Ready. 35. "And one, and two." 36. "And three, and four."

    The Fourth Position is one of the most difficult in which to achieve a good *demi-plié,* so practice it very carefully. Be sure that both shoulders and both hips face straight front. Watch that you do not "sit" in the hip on the side of the foot which is in back. The spine must be kept straight. The foot in back will want to roll in and the knee will want to fall in front of the arch, so you must be careful not to let this happen. You can overcome this by making sure that your weight is kept even over both feet. Don't worry if you can't turn your feet outward as far as the girl in the drawing. Do the best you can correctly, and if you practice faithfully, your turn-out will improve gradually but surely.

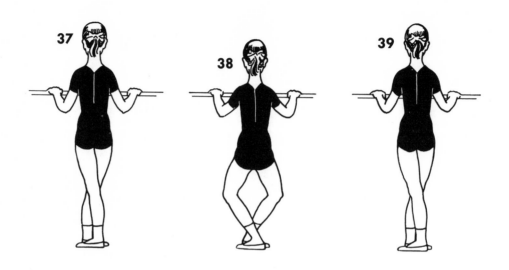

DEMI-PLIÉ IN FIFTH POSITION

37. Ready. 38. "And one, and two." 39. "And three, and four."

Be sure that as you bend your knees you keep lifting up out of your hips.

We practice the *plié* in order to make the muscles and ligaments of our legs very limber and supple. They must become like elastic, especially at the knees, so that they stretch and then return to their normal position readily and respond instantly when you want to move.

All ballet dancers practice their *pliés* constantly, and no professional dancer would think of beginning to practice or dance on the stage without first "warming up" with *plié* exercises. You must do this too.

THE GRAND PLIÉ (grahn plee-ay')

Do not practice the *grand plié* until your teacher tells you that you do a good *demi-plié* and may now begin learning the *grand plié*. This is very important because if you cannot hold all the proper body placement in the *demi-plié* you will never be able to do so in the *grand plié*.

Remember not to let your seat stick out, not to sit into the hips, not to drop the ribs. The lower your knees bend, the taller you grow out of your hips, as though someone were lifting you by the crown of your head. Keep pressing your knees back and out so you feel the stretch in your hips. Watch carefully that all the toes remain on the floor even when the heels lift. Don't try to improve your turn-out by pushing your heels further front as you bend; keep your feet in exactly the same position you had when you started.

GRAND PLIÉ IN FIRST POSITION

40. 41. 42. 43. Take four slow counts to bend the knees, and four slow counts to straighten them.

When you allow your heels to lift off the floor, after first doing a good *demi-plié*, just allow them to raise slightly. Do not go way up on your toes. Come back up just as slowly as you went down and through the same stages, so you pass through a good *demi-plié* before your knees straighten.

Remember not to get "set" in your knees by dropping too quickly and sitting in the *plié* and then jumping up quickly. Count slowly four counts down and four counts up.

GRAND PLIÉ IN SECOND POSITION

44. 45. 46. 47. Take four slow counts to bend the knees, and four slow counts to straighten them.

The heel should never be allowed to leave the floor in doing the *grand plié* in Second Position. Do not bend the knees any deeper than you can while still holding a good position with everything correctly placed.

GRAND PLIÉ IN THIRD POSITION

48. 49. 50. 51. Take four slow counts to bend the knees, and four slow counts to straighten them.

This position need not be practiced except as a substitute for Fifth Position if that is too difficult for you at this time.

GRAND PLIÉ IN FOURTH POSITION

52. 53. 54. 55. Take four slow counts to bend the knees, and four slow counts to straighten them.

Take care that both knees stay at the same level all through the *plié* and both the heels are the same height off the floor. You do this by keeping your weight even over both feet. Don't let that back foot and knee roll in!

GRAND PLIÉ IN FIFTH POSITION

56. 57. 58. 59. Take four slow counts to bend the knees, and four slow counts to straighten them.

Be sure to keep your heels in a straight line with your toes and as you bend keep them firmly in place, even though they lift up. Do not let your feet slip out of position so your heels turn back and your toes turn front.

60. 61. Don't do this!

CORRECT POSITION STANDING
AT THE BARRE

In all the following exercises the distance between you and the barre is very important, because it has a definite effect upon your body placement as you work.

You must stand close enough to the barre to keep your hand on it slightly in front of you at all times. Your axis line (imaginary line running from crown to toes) must always remain straight. If you are too far from the barre and have to reach for it, you will be pulled "off center." If you stand too close to the barre, your arm will force your shoulder to hunch in an ugly fashion. Test this out for yourself until you find just the correct distance for comfort and good placement.

62. Too far from the barre.

63. Too close to the barre.

64. Correct position at the barre.

POSITION OF THE FREE ARM AND HAND AT THE BARRE

65. The arm in *seconde* position.

66. Note the grouping of the fingers. Thumb and third finger indented. When the arm is raised in Second Position, keep the elbow up and don't "break" at the wrist, but keep the hand in line with the arm.

PORT DE BRAS AT THE BARRE
(por deh brah)

Port de bras is the carriage of the arms. This port de bras at the barre is used as a preparation for all of the exercises that follow. It is very good to become accustomed to using the arm, and to holding it in Second Position as you work. Pay particular attention to the head, as the angle at which you hold your head is very important.

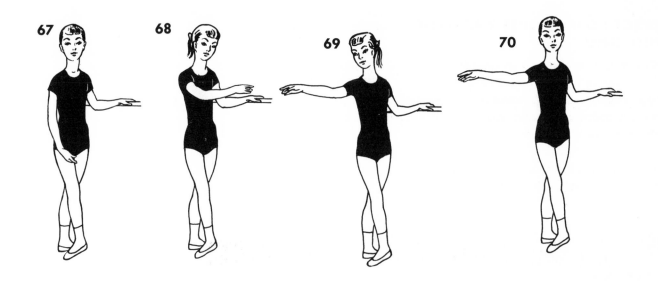

67. Stand still, ready to begin.

68. Raise the arm as high as your chest. Keep it round. Let your head incline a little toward the barre, look at the palm of your hand. Count, "And one . . ."

69. Open the arm to the side (Second Position). Keep the elbow lifted and slightly rounded. Follow the hand with your eyes so your head turns. Count, "And two."

70. Turn your head front and look straight out, ready to begin the exercise.

CORRECT POSITION OF THE FOOT
IN POINTING

71. CORRECT: In pointing straight front (Fourth Position, front) try to keep the foot in its correct line with the leg, which is open (or turned out) from the hip. The heel is pressed forward and up and the point is on the big toe, not the little one.

72. INCORRECT: Don't sickle the foot, that is, press the toes out of line with the heel.

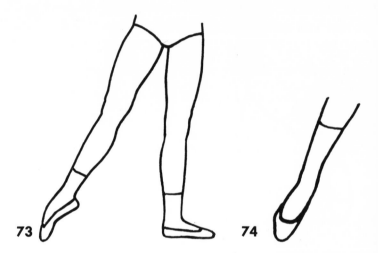

73   74

71   72

73. CORRECT: In pointing to the side (Second Position) again be sure that the foot is held in its proper "alignment" to the leg, that is, keep the foot on a straight line with the leg. Lift up the heel and point up on the tips of the toes.

74. INCORRECT: Don't allow the heel to turn back.

75. INCORRECT: Don't allow the heel to get out of line with the toes.

76. INCORRECT: Don't bend your toes over to point so that you press on the knuckles.

 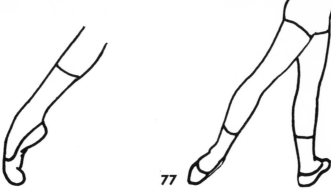 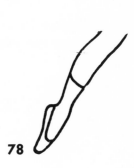

75   76   77   78

77. CORRECT: In pointing back (Fourth Position, back) rest on the inside of the big toe and press the heel down.

78. INCORRECT: Don't turn the foot in and let the heel stick up in the air.

BATTEMENTS TENDUS (baht-mahn' tahn-doo')

Every exercise you do at the barre has a special pur pose. That is why it is so important to practice them co rectly. If you do them only halfway, you won't get th benefits or the results you wish and expect.

Before you start each exercise take time to make sur that you are standing properly according to the principle of body placement. Test yourself to see if you are ba anced forward over the balls of your feet by teetering u and down on your toes and letting go of the barre. The put your hand back on the barre in its right place an hold the barre lightly. Be sure to stay this way all throug the exercise.

Check yourself to make sure that your hips are facin straight front and are both even. See if your shoulder are both front and pressed down and relaxed.

The *battement tendu* will make your feet and legs ver strong and will develop a beautiful, arched instep in you feet.

Practice it at first only from the First Position until yo get the feel of it. Practice doing it "*à la quatrième devant*" (to the Fourth Position front), "*à la seconde*" (to Secon Position, or side), "*à la quatrième derrière*" (to the Fourt Position back). As you practice, be sure your weight is cen tered over the ball of your supporting foot. Don't put an weight on the pointing foot.

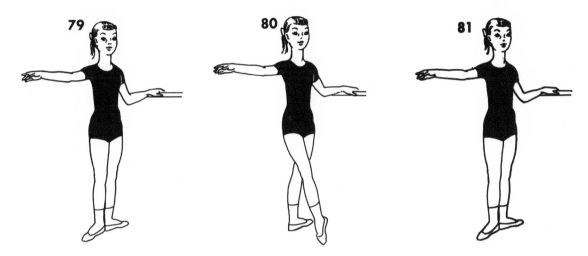

BATTEMENTS TENDUS À LA QUATRIÈME
DEVANT (baht-mahn' tahn-doo' ah lah caht-ree-em' deh-vahn')

Prepare with the *port de bras* as in 67 through 70.

79. Ready to begin. Left hand on barre.

80. Slide the right foot forward in a straight line as far as you can reach without getting "off center" or letting your right hip go front. Keep both knees pulled up tight. Keep the heel of the pointing foot on the floor until the last possible moment so that there is a feeling of resistance in the leg as it slides out to point. Count, "And one . . ."

81. Return the foot to First Position, sliding it back in the same manner, with the knees pulled up very tight. Be sure that your feet are not rolling in or out and that the arch of the supporting foot is lifted, because you are holding the floor firmly with ALL of your toes. Count, "And two."

Practice this exercise 8 times with the right foot, then turn around and do it 8 times with the left foot.

BATTEMENTS TENDUS À LA SECONDE (ah lah seh-cohnd')

82. Ready. 83. "And one." 84. "And two."

This exercise is the same as *battement tendu à la quatrième devant* except that it is executed *à la seconde* (to the side). Slide the right foot out in a direct line from the left heel. Don't let the right hip raise up. Point the foot in line with the leg, heel directly under. If your seat is under and your stomach pulled up, your leg will turn out **better.**

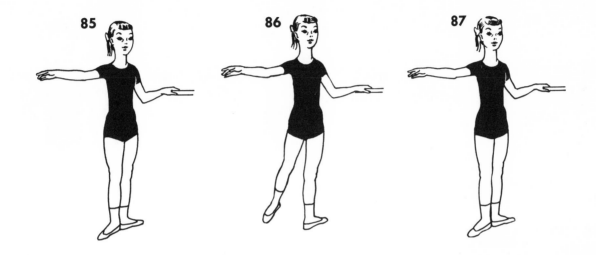

BATTEMENTS TENDUS À LA QUATRIÈME DERRIÈRE
(ah lah caht-ree-em′ dair-ee-air′)

85. Ready. 86. "And one." 87. "And two."

Here again is the *battement tendu,* executed to Fourth Position back instead of to the front or side. Slide the right foot straight back in line with the left heel. Watch carefully that both the hips and the shoulders are facing front. Although you are trying to keep the right hip front and in line with the left hip, be careful that it does not drop forward and turn your leg in.

88. 89. What's wrong with these pictures? I hope you don't look like this!

88   89

90

BATTEMENTS TENDUS À LA SECONDE FROM FIFTH POSITION

When you begin to get the "feel" of the *battements tendus* as you practice them from First Position, that is, when you are able to slide your whole foot out till it points and slide it back to First Position again with perfectly straight knees, then you are ready to begin practicing this exercise from Fifth Position. Begin by taking it only "*à la seconde*" (pointing directly to the side in Second Position).

If you cannot turn your legs outward sufficiently to take Fifth Position without rolling over on your instep, practice the exercise from Third Position until your turn-out improves enough to permit a fairly good Fifth Position.

Stand with your left hand on the barre, feet in Fifth Position with the right foot front. Prepare with a *port de bras* as in 67 through 70.

90. Ready to begin. Check yourself for correct posture, weight forward over the balls of the feet.

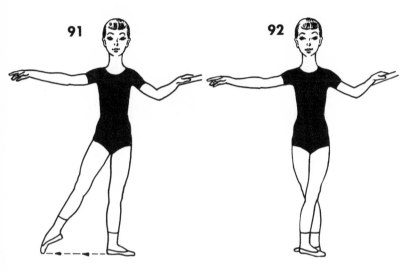

91. Count, "And one . . ." Your toes lead out in a straight line. Remember to slide the whole foot out, the heel remains on the floor till the last possible moment.

92. Count, "And two." Your heel leads in, in a straight line into Fifth Position in back of the left foot. Place the heel firmly on the floor.

Repeat the slide out to the point, then into Fifth Position, closing the left foot in front of the right foot. Repeat the entire exercise 16 times, closing the working foot alternately in back and in front of the supporting foot. Turn around and repeat the exercise 16 times with the left foot.

Remember not to put any weight on the pointing foot. Keep both knees pulled up tight and straight at all times. Reach out as far as you can (without getting off center) with the toes of the pointing foot.

BATTEMENTS TENDUS À LA SECONDE WITH DEMI-PLIÉ IN FIFTH POSITION

This exercise is excellent to prepare you for jumping steps so that you will have a good *ballon* or bounce in your jumping. It is done like the simple *battement tendu à la seconde*, but the knees bend outward in a *demi-plié* each time the foot closes to Fifth Position. When you are able to do this correctly pointing *à la seconde*, you may also practice it pointing *à la quatrième devant* and *à la quatrième derrière*.

Begin by standing at the proper distance from the barre, left hand on the barre, feet in Fifth Position with the right foot front. Prepare with a *port de bras* as in 67 through 70.

93. Slide the right foot out to point in Second Position. Count, "And one . . ." Both knees are pulled up tightly so that they are very straight.

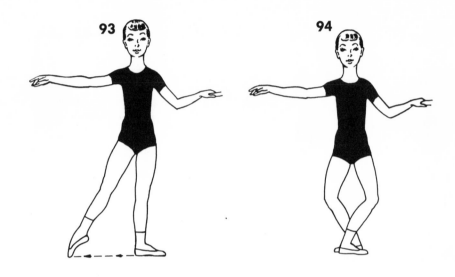

94. Slide the right foot into Fifth Position behind the left foot. As you slide the right foot in, bend both knees slowly so that when you arrive in Fifth Position both knees are bent in a *demi-plié*. Count, "And two."

Take care not to roll in on your insteps. Keep the little toes firmly on the floor; both heels must be kept very straight and the body lifted up out of the hips; keep the knees directly over the toes.

Straighten both knees slowly, at the same time, as you slide the right foot out to point again in Second Position, so that when you arrive at the pointed position both knees are pulled up tight.

Practice this exercise 16 times with each foot.

95

BATTEMENTS DÉGAGÉS (baht-mahn' day-gah-zhay')

This exercise will make your ankles very supple and will develop speed in your feet so that when you jump your feet will always be pointed beautifully. It is also important because it forms part of jumping steps such as *sissonne*, which you will learn later as you advance in ballet technique, and because it will help you in *batterie*, or beaten steps, which are part of advanced allegro work.

Work slowly and carefully as you practice it now.

95. Ready. Stand in First Position with the left hand on the barre. Check yourself for correct posture and good placement. Have the right arm curved and held down in front of you. Keep it there during the exercise. Incline your head slightly to the right shoulder and leave it there through the exercise.

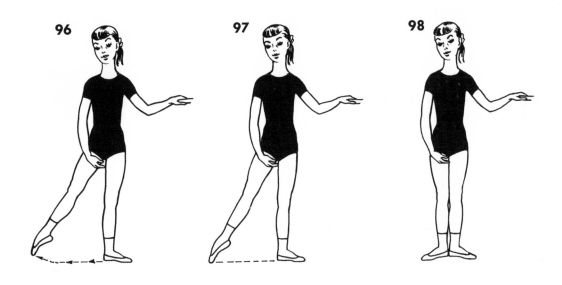

96. Slide the entire right foot out as in *battement tendu*, but as you point the foot allow the toes to raise up off the floor about three inches. Point very strongly. Count, "And one . . ."

97. Lower the toes of the right foot to the floor in Second Position. Count, "And two . . ."

98. Slide the right foot on the floor into perfect First Position. Count, "And three . . ." Hold First Position for count "And four."

These four counts comprise the exercise. Repeat it 16 times with each foot.

RONDS DE JAMBE À TERRE, EN DEHORS
(rawn deh zhamb ah tair, ahn deh-or')

This exercise will do more than any other to loosen and limber your hip ligaments so that your turn-out will improve and your legs will become more free so that you can raise them more easily and higher off the floor.

As in all the exercises, you must stand absolutely still with the weight of the body over the ball of the supporting foot. As the working leg describes the semicircle, do not turn your hips or shoulders. Keep them facing straight front at all times.

Stand at the correct distance from the barre. Left hand on the barre, feet in First Position. Prepare with a *port de bras* as in 67 through 70.

99. Ready to begin. Perfect posture and placement, head erect, eyes looking straight forward.

100. Slide the right foot front to point in Fourth Position, as in *battement tendu*. Point the foot very strongly and keep the heel forward and up. Count, "And one..."

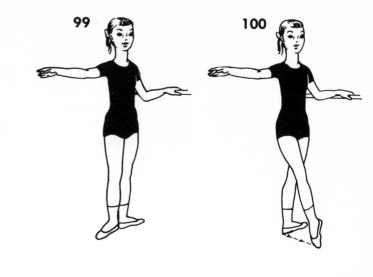

101. Slide the toes of the right foot around on the floor to point in Second Position. Keep the foot straight as you point. Count, "And two..."

102. Slide the toes of the right foot around on the floor to point in Fourth Position back. Remember to rest on the inside of the big toe with the heel pressed down. Count, "And three..."

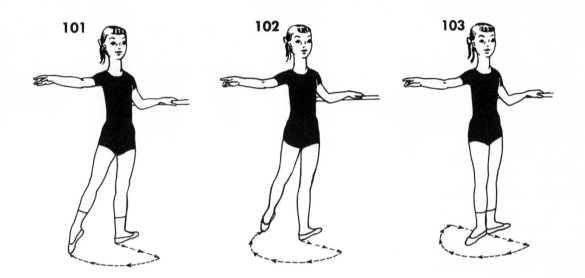

101 **102** **103**

103. Slide the right foot on the floor into perfect First Position. Be careful to straighten the foot so that the little toe and the big toe are both on the floor as the foot slides in. Count, "And four."

Repeat the entire exercise 8 times with each foot. Work slowly, pausing in each position so that your placement through the hips will be correct and your foot positions will be turned out with the foot properly aligned to the leg. (*See 71 through 73.*)

RONDS DE JAMBE À TERRE, EN DEDANS
(ahn deh-dahn')

You do this exactly as I have described the outward circles of the leg, but reverse the movement of the foot. After the *port de bras* preparation point the right foot to Fourth Position back on count "One," then slide the toes around to Second Position on count "two," slide the toes to Fourth Position front on "three," and return the foot to perfect First Position on "four."

Do this exercise 8 times with each foot.

PORT DE BRAS AU CORPS CAMBRÉ
(por deh brah oh cor cahm-bray')

This is an important exercise to practice because it will stretch the muscles and ligaments of your back and thighs and knees. At the same time it will help you to acquire graceful movements of the arms and head.

104. Ready. Stand in Fifth Position (you may stand in First Position for the first few months) with the right foot front and the left hand on the barre.

105. Bend forward from the hips. Keep your ribs well lifted up even though you are bending forward. Do not allow your knees to bend, but as you stretch forward pull your knees up tighter. Be careful to stay forward over the balls of the feet and not to pull back into the heels. Reach for the floor with your right hand. Count slowly and bend slowly. Count, "And one, and two . . ."

106. Straighten up. The right arm is stretched forward in front of your chest. Count, "And three . . ."

107. Raise the right arm up higher so that it is over your head. Be careful not to allow the right shoulder to hunch up. Look up toward your hand. Count, "And four . . ."

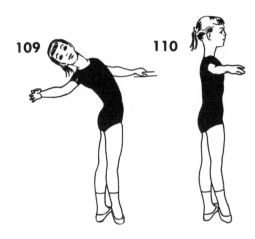

109 **110**

DON'T DO THIS!

111

108. Bend straight back from the hips. As you do so, push your seat forward and keep pulling up tightly on the knees. Allow the head to drop back. Count, "And five, and six . . ."

109. Open the right arm out to Second Position and turn your head to the right so that you are looking at your hand. Count, "And seven . . ."

110. Straighten up. Count, "And eight."

    Repeat this exercise 4 times on each side.

111. Don't pull back into the heels as you bend forward.

112

112. Don't bend back from the waist, letting the seat stick out in back.

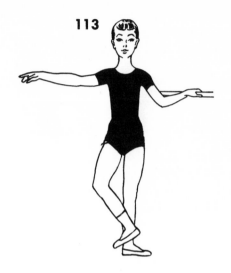

113

BATTEMENTS FRAPPÉS (baht-mahn' frah-pay')

This is another very important exercise for you to practice carefully and slowly. It will develop great strength in the insteps of your feet and in your thighs. Another reason why it is important for you to learn this step correctly is that it forms part of the jumping step called *jeté*.

Stand in Fifth Position with the right foot front and the left hand on the barre. As you do your *port de bras* preparation raise your right foot to a flexed position on your left ankle.

113. Ready. Your right heel is crossed in front of your left anklebone. The foot is not pointed but flexed, that is, it forms a right angle to your leg. Don't allow the toes to stick up or to curl down, keep them softly pressed downward. Remember to stand up tall out of your hips and do not "sit" in the left hip. Keep the weight forward over the ball of the left foot; press the right knee out and back; try to open from the hip as much as possible.

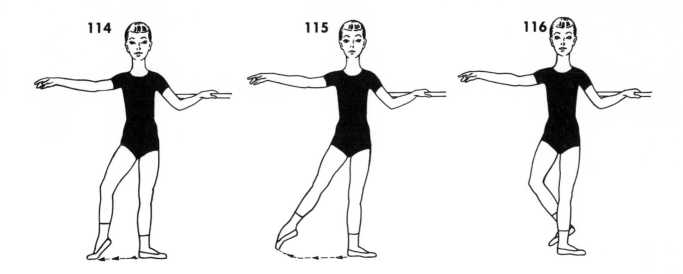

114   115   116

14. Brush the right foot downward and outward so that the ball of the foot strikes the floor. Count, "And . . ."

15. Point the right foot hard and at the same time snap the right knee straight. Allow the toes to be about three inches off the floor. Count, "One . . ."

16. Bend the right knee and bring the right foot to rest in back of the left ankle. Cross the right heel to the anklebone. Count, "And two."

Practice this exercise slowly 16 times with each foot. Alternate, crossing in front and in back of the supporting ankle. Use strength in thrusting the foot out. This is not a weak movement. Be sure to strike the ball of the foot on the floor each time. The only movement of the exercise takes place in the knee and ankle joints. NEVER raise or lower your thigh.

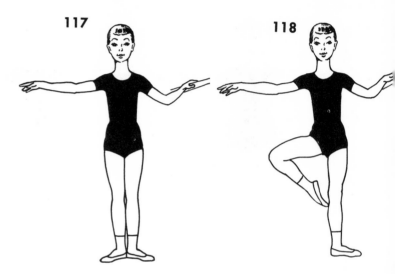

117

118

BATTEMENTS RETIRÉS (baht-mahn' reh-teer-ay')

This exercise is a basic movement of ballet technique and will strengthen you for adagio (slow and controlled movements and extensions of the legs). Practice it with great care so that you work correctly through your hips. Do not allow the hip to raise up when the knee lifts, but press the hip down so that both hips remain straight and even. At the same time lift yourself tall out of both hips.

Stand in First Position with the left hand on the barre. Prepare with a *port de bras* as in 67 through 70.

117. Ready. Check your posture and placement. You seat must be well under and the stomach well lifted

118. Draw the right foot up the side of the left leg unti the toes of the right foot touch the little hollow a the side of the left knee. Keep the right foot wel pointed so the heel is far away from the left leg Open the right knee as far back as possible. Re member not to let your hip go up, press the righ hip down so it stays even with the left hip. Hol

119

your weight forward over the ball of your left foot; don't pull back into the left heel. Be very careful that your right foot is pointing straight—press the heel front and the toes back so that the foot does not "sickle" (point crooked). Count, "And one . . ." as the foot raises up. Hold the position on "And two . . ."

119. Return the right foot to First Position on count "And three . . ." Hold First Position on "And four."

Repeat the exercise 8 times with each foot.

120. Don't do this!

120

GRANDS BATTEMENTS (grahn baht-mahn')

The *grands battements* will make you more limber so that you can move your legs more freely. It will make the muscles of your back and stomach very strong, too, if you work to control each movement and remember to hold yourself properly as you work.

Although the drawings show this exercise from Fifth Position, you should practice it from First Position for the first few months until you are able to do good *battements tendus* from Fifth Position, because the *battement tendu* is the basis of this exercise. The drawings have purposely been made without extreme turn-out. This is to remind you not to turn your feet out more than you are able to do with the entire leg from the hip joint.

For the beginner, in order to achieve straight knees and good posture, it is wise to practice this exercise in four counts. Later, when you have been dancing for about a year, you will take the leg up and down without the pauses.

GRANDS BATTEMENTS À LA QUATRIÈME DEVANT

Stand in First Position or Fifth Position with the right foot front, left hand on the barre. Prepare with a *port de bras* as in 67 through 70.

121. Ready. Check for posture and placement.

122. Slide the right foot front to point in Fourth Position, as in *battement tendu*. Count, "One . . ."

123. Raise the right leg up as high as you can while keeping both hips in line and even. You will have to pull the right hip back a little because if it goes forward when the leg raises, your leg will be turned in. Stretch your right leg so the knee is very straight. Pull the supporting knee up tight. Lift up your stom-

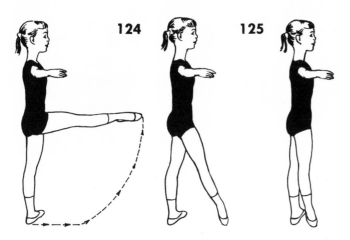

123   **124**   **125**

ach and your ribs so that you are very tall. Try to raise the leg as high as your hips, but do not bend forward or back to get it up. Keep both shoulders straight and low. Count, "Two . . ."

124. Lower the right toes to the floor in Fourth Position; don't put any weight on them. Count, "Three . . ."

125. Slide the right foot back to First Position or Fifth Position in front of the left foot. "And four." Be sure not to bend the right knee.

126. 127. Don't do this!

126   **127**

GRANDS BATTEMENTS À LA SECONDE

This is a most difficult exercise. It is especially hard to keep your correct placement in this exercise, but you must try very hard to do so or the exercise has no value for you.

If you remember not to throw your weight onto the working foot, it will help you. All the weight must remain over the ball of the supporting foot at all times and the working leg must go up and down without any help from any other part of the body. Keep your shoulders facing straight front, very relaxed, and pressed down low in the back. Don't let them hunch up when you raise your leg. Keep both of your hips facing straight front and even. Don't twist outward from the barre. Your spine must be very straight all through the exercise.

Hold your head erect and look straight ahead. I hope you have not forgotten to do this on all the exercises as you practiced; your head is a very important member of your body and your eyes play a big part in your balance.

Stand in First Position or in Fifth Position with the right foot in front of the left foot. Prepare with a *port de bras*.

128. Ready. Check for posture and placement.

129. Slide the right foot out to point in Second Position as in *battement tendu*. Count, "One . . ."

130. Raise the right leg. Be careful not to lean to the right or the left or to move in your shoulders. Press the right hip down, as the leg comes up, so that it stays even with the left hip. Keep both knees pulled up tight and straight. Press your seat under and hold the heel forward. Count, "Two . . ."

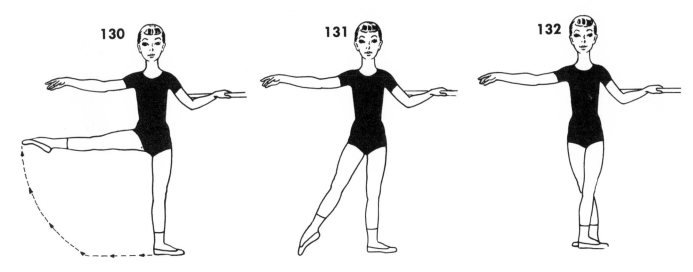

130 **131** **132**

131. Lower the toes to the floor in Second Position. Don't put any weight on them. Count, "Three . . ."

132. Slide the right foot into First Position or Fifth Position in back of the left foot. Count, "Four." Don't allow the knees to bend to come into position.

Do this exercise 8 times with each leg. If you are practicing it from Fifth Position, close the right foot alternately in back and in front of the left foot.

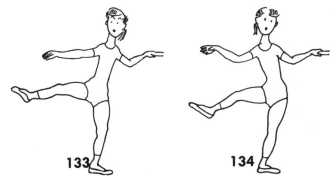

133 **134**

133. 134. Don't do this!

135

136

GRANDS BATTEMENTS À LA QUATRIÈME DERRIÈRE

Practice this exercise facing the barre. Center your weight over the ball of the supporting foot and do not rock back and forth as your leg moves up and down. Hold your shoulders at their normal position; do not press them back. Hold your ribs up, but don't sway your back. Keep your head erect; do not look down.

135. Ready. Both hands holding the barre lightly. Check for posture and placement. Stand in First Position or in Fifth Position with the right foot in back of the left foot.

136. Slide the right foot back to point in Fourth Position. Keep your weight forward over the ball of the left foot. Both shoulders straight front. Count, "One . . ."

137. Raise the right leg up. Do not allow the weight to fall back into the left heel, press forward. Keep both knees pulled up tight and straight. Don't press your shoulders back; hold them naturally and be sure that the right shoulder is in line with the left shoulder. Don't drop your head; look straight ahead. Count, "Two . . ."

138. Lower the toes to the floor. Do not put any weight on them. Count, "Three . . ."

139. Slide the right foot into First Position or Fifth Position in back of the left foot. Count, "Four."

Repeat this exercise 8 times with each foot.

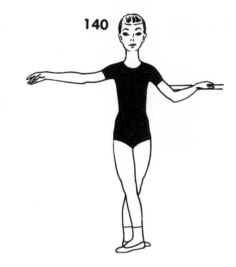

140

BATTEMENTS SOUTENUS, À LA SECONDE
(baht-mahn' soo-ten-oo')

This exercise is especially valuable to improve the step called *assemblé,* which is one of the basic allegro steps of ballet. As you practice it, be very conscious of the position of your hips so that you do not "sit" in the hip over the supporting leg or allow the hip on the side of the working leg to push out of line. Be perfectly "centered." Watch carefully that you do not roll inward on the arch of your foot as you *plié;* keep the knee directly over the toes and the spine very straight.

Stand in Fifth Position (or in First if you are not yet ready for Fifth) with the right foot in front of the left. Prepare with a *port de bras* as in **67** through **70**.

140. Ready. Check for posture and placement.

141. Slide the right foot out to point in Second Position and as it slides out allow the left knee to bend in a good *demi-plié.* Keep your head erect; don't turn your shoulders away from front. Count, "And one . . ."

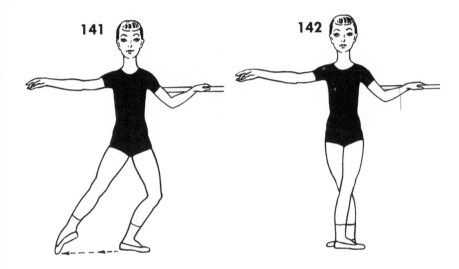

141 **142**

142. Slide the right foot into Fifth Position (or First Position) in back of the left foot and at the same time straighten the left knee so that both knees are pulled up tight and straight as you finish. Count, "And two."

Practice this exercise 16 times with each foot. If you are working from Fifth Position, close the right foot alternately in back and in front of the left foot.

143. Don't do this!

143

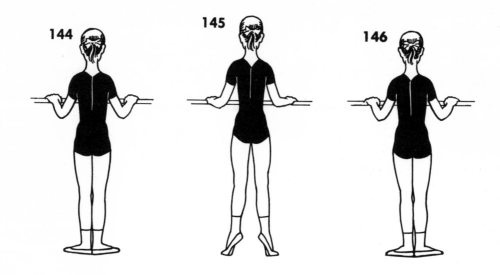

144 **145** **146**

RELEVÉS (reh-leh-vay')

144. In First Position: Ready. Face the barre. Hold it lightly with both hands. Check yourself for perfect posture and placement. Keep the head erect and look straight forward. Turn your legs outward only as far as you can without straining to keep from rolling in on the arches. Pull the knees up tight.

145. Rise on the balls of the feet pulling the heels straight

up through the ankle, knees still very straight. Press the balls of the feet into the floor and feel all of your toes on the floor. Count, "And one, and two . . ."

146. Lower the heels gently and very slowly to the floor, pulling the knees up tightly as you do so. Count, "And three, and four." Take the whole two counts to lower the heels.

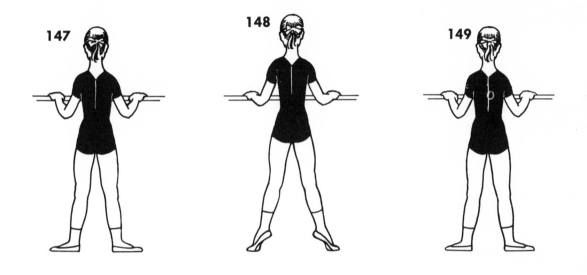

147

148

149

Practice these *relevés* in First Position 8 times, and then do the same thing in Second Position 8 times.

147. Ready.

148. "And one, and two . . ."

149. "And three, and four."

These *relevés* are meant to develop strength in your feet, ankles, and legs. They will help you to jump better in allegro steps and will prepare you for dancing *sur les pointes* (on the toes). Practice them slowly and with great care for posture and placement.

GLOSSARY

Correct placement: the correct way to hold the body for ballet so as to develop good balance, good form, good line, and ease of execution.

À la quatrième derrière (*ah lah caht-ree-em' dair-ee-air'*): to Fourth Position back.

À la quatrième devant (*ah lah caht-ree-em' deh-vahn'*): to Fourth Position front.

À la seconde (*ah lah seh-cohnd'*): to Second Position.

À terre (*ah tair*): on the floor.

Battement (*baht-mahn'*): a beating action of the leg.

Battement dégagé (*baht-mahn' day-gah-zhay'*): disengaged beating of the leg.

Battement frappé (*baht-mahn' frah-pay'*): struck beating of the leg.

Battement retiré (*baht-mahn' reh-teer-ay'*): pulled up or shortened beating of the leg.

Battement soutenu (*baht-mahn' soo-ten-oo'*): beating of the leg held under.

Battement tendu (*baht-mahn' tahn-doo'*): stretched beating of the leg.

Cambré (*cahm-bray'*): arched.

Demi-plié (*deh'-mee plee-ay'*): half bend. To bend the knees as far as possible with the heels firmly on the floor and the body correctly placed.

En dedans (*ahn deh-dahn'*): inward.

En dehors (*ahn deh-or'*): outward.

Grand battement (*grahn baht-mahn'*): large beating of the leg.

Grand plié (*grahn plee-ay'*): deep or full bend, allowing the heels to rise from the floor (except in Second Position) and bending as low as the knees permit.

Plié (*plee-ay'*): meaning "bent." In ballet, to bend the knees.

Port de bras (*por deh brah*): the carriage or use of the arms in ballet.

Port de bras au corps cambré (*por deh brah oh cor cahm-bray'*): carriage of the arms with bending of the body.

Relevé (*reh-leh-vay'*): to rise to the *demi-pointe*, or half toe.

Ronds de jambe (*rawn deh zhamb*): circles of the leg.